pebble
mosaics

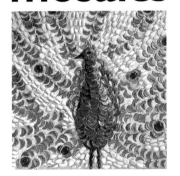

pebble mosaics

Step-by-step projects
for inside & out

Ann Frith

David & Charles

PICTURE CREDITS
Tony Gervis/Robert Harding, p7 top and bottom; p11 top left
Richard McNabb/Irish Stock Library, p8
Maggie Howith's garden/John Glover; p9

A DAVID & CHARLES BOOK

First published in the UK in 2002
First paperback edition 2004
Reprinted 2005

Text copyright © Ann Frith 2002, 2004
Photography and layout copyright © David & Charles 2002, 2004

Distributed in North America
by F&W Publications, Inc.
4700 East Galbraith Road
Cincinnati, OH 45236
1-800-289-0963

A catalogue record for this book is available from the British Library.

ISBN 0 7153 1186 7 hardback
ISBN 0 7153 1899 3 paperback

Printed in China by SNP Leefung
for David & Charles
Brunel House   Newton Abbot   Devon

The author has made every effort to ensure that all the instructions in this book are
accurate and safe, and therefore cannot accept liability for any resulting injury, damage
or loss to persons or property however it may arise. When working with electrically
powered water fountains, always follow the manufacturer's instructions and adhere to
the safety precautions. If in doubt, consult a qualified electrician.

contents

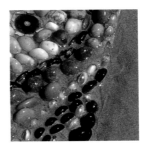

introduction

Who hasn't strolled along a pebbly beach, plucking the odd treasure from the tideline as the waves reveal the beauty of the stones? While it is illegal to remove pebbles from a beach or a river bank without prior permission, there is a myriad of other sources from which you can legitimately acquire them. The growth of interest in garden design has encouraged garden centres and interior stores to stock a wide variety of different materials. Pebbles of every size and shape and the more exotic polished versions can all be used to delightful effect. In addition, other materials provide vivid colour to complement the more subtle tones of the pebbles. Materials such as glass, slate, ceramic, mosaic tiles and terracotta all have their place.

pebble mosaics of the past

The history of pebble mosaic stretches back into antiquity. The earliest known examples were unearthed at Gordium, near Ankara in Turkey. Dating from the eighth century BC, they show figures made with light pebbles against a darker background. Although they are rather stiff and awkward, they show how people were using a natural material for both practical and decorative purposes.

The Greeks took pebble mosaics to new levels of sophistication and examples are found throughout the stretches of their empire: as far west as Sicily and in the east in the Greek colonies of the Crimea. Some of the best surviving examples can be seen in Pella and Olinthos in Macedonian northern Greece.

At the Olinthos site, which dates from the fifth century BC, the development of pebble art is clearly illustrated. The background of the design is black or blue-black, with the figures in white or off-white making a striking tableau. Animals and people are represented in a lively and realistic manner. The pebbles, which are 1–2cm (½–¾in) long, are much more uniform in shape than earlier pebble mosaics, adding to the texture without distracting the eye. However, intricate areas such as faces have been rendered in much smaller pebbles to give more detail. Another device is to outline motifs with some tiny pebbles.

The pebble-mosaic floors in Pella, dating from the fourth century BC, show a significant development of the pebble technique. Here, new materials have been introduced to make up for the limitations of pebbles. These designs are so sophisticated to be almost equal to wall paintings. To overcome the problems of a limited pebble palette, artifical pebbles were made and painted, predominantly in reds and greens. Another stylistic device is also evident: instead of just

left and below: Two examples from the House of Lion, Pella, Greece, showing a contrast between strikingly simple geometric squares and more sophisticated, intricate designs.

outlining the figures in a contrasting colour, long strips of terracotta and lead wire were used to add more detail. The pebbles continued to get smaller, allowing greater and greater detail to be added. In the third century BC, these pebble mosaics led to the development of tile mosaic and the decline of the pebble art.

Nevertheless, pebble mosaics appear in many other locations throughout the world. Some of the most beautiful appear as the result of the Islamic influence in Moorish Spain. Here, gardens were enhanced by intricately patterned paths, pebble mosaics being eminently suitable for the geometric and flowing patterns that are part of Islamic decorative style. This tradition has continued, long after the demise of the Islamic empire, and today many examples can still be seen in southern Spain.

Throughout history there have been two main types of pebble mosaics. Domestic styles, using pebbles from local rivers and beaches, were employed for hard surfaces around houses and as roads. Many have simple patterns and motifs incorporated in them to enhance entrances. The other type includes grand, elaborate designs. Many of these drew on classical Greek themes. Italian Garden designers working during the Renaissance incorporated pebble mosaics in their designs. These in turn influenced northern European gardens and houses and, as a result, we see pebble mosaic in the estates of the wealthy throughout Europe.

Modern pebble mosaics are not yet common sights, although the recent growth of interest in all areas of gardening has made many more materials available to the pebble-mosaic designer. Most recent examples draw on or reproduce traditional patterns. The exception to these in Britain is Maggie Howarth who is, almost single-handedly, reviving the art. Her stunning, elaborate designs are an inspiration to all amateur pebblers. Birds, fish and other beasts leap into life. Maggie has spent years collecting suitable pebbles and her work is a testimony to her feel for pattern and texture. Other inspiring exponents of the art are Roberto Burle Marx in Brazil (Copacabana beach), Eduardo Nery in Portugal (Lisbon) and Raphael Gimenez in Spain (Cordoba).

above: One of Maggie Howarth's contemporary designs at Hilltop, Lancashire, England.
opposite: Bold, geometric patterns were used for a grand garden at Powerscourt House, Co. Wicklow, Ireland.

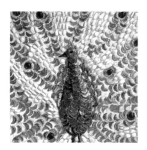   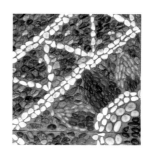

creating your own work

In this book, the projects have been graded from very simple ones to more elaborate ideas that require careful planning, more work and greater confidence. This allows you to build your skills, step by step, by working through the book. If you are a little nervous, start with a simple project, but if you like a challenge start anywhere you like.

However, if all of this inspires you to create your own designs, don't be afraid to experiment and create your own ideas. If you have an idea for a mosaic, try it. There is not one 'right' way. If it works and looks good, fantastic; if it falls apart or looks awkward your next one will be better as you will have learned something. Pieces are rarely

complete failures; remember the good bits for next time. If a material or way of doing something is not included in the book it doesn't mean you can't do it.

Equally, designing can be achieved in many ways. Much of my work has started with a very basic idea: maybe a flower, or the pattern on a feather. Keep it simple: too much detail in the shapes, patterns or even colours will detract from the stones and become muddled. Remember that contrasts in design look good, both in pebble size and shade. Draw inspiration from things around you: a stylish pattern on a plate or a rug may give you ideas. Look at images for children: many

left: A classical wave design found in the Pella mosaics (far left) has been used in the Fountain Swirl (see page 74).

are bright and bold, simplifying shapes and erasing excess detail. If you are not happy about drawing, cheat! Trace, photocopy, and cut out bits to make your design.

Mosaics made from tiles are readily transferred to pebbles, provided the design can be seen clearly. Examples in museums and books will provide rich hunting grounds for ideas and inspiration.

When selecting pebbles, choose smooth, rounded, evenly shaped ones and group them by colour. A variety of pebbles will add considerable interest to your mosaic. Each shape will suit a different pattern. For example, round pebbles are ideal for flower centres whilst longer pebbles will be perfect for petals. You will soon learn to select according to shape as well as colour.

My hope is that this book will give you hours of interest, creating beautiful objects to give you pleasure and satisfaction for years to come.

Good luck and happy mosaicing!

Ann Frith

simple
designs

upstream

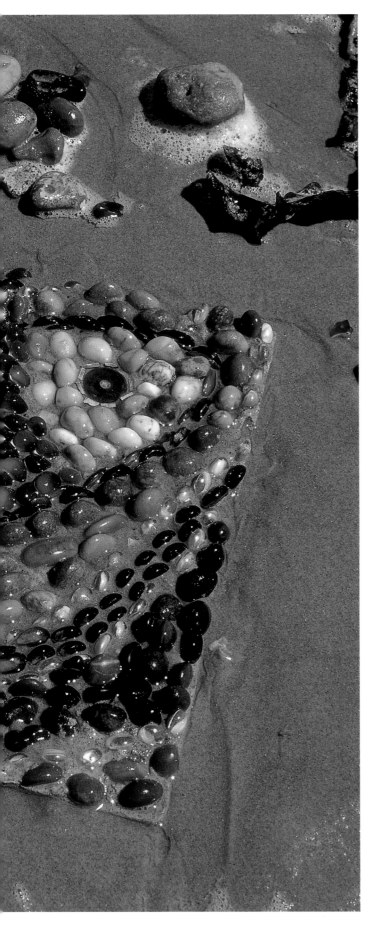

Here is an ideal project for the pebble-mosaic novice. It is made in a plastic tray, from ordinary cement reinforced with chicken wire. A design is drawn in the wet cement, and pebbles, glass and slate are carefully pressed in.

Pebbles have a natural affinity with marine subjects. To provide strong visual interest, the fish itself incorporates a variety of different materials: cut slate (in this case an old roofing tile), smooth white pebbles and glass nuggets.

Notice how the lines of pebbles around the outside of the fish give it movement by describing the contours of its body. Making bands of darker or lighter pebbles will give the background more interest. Don't be afraid to experiment!

upstream steps

materials

chicken wire
cement and coarse sand
  (or ready-mixed sand
  and cement)
flat glass discs (or beads)
slate
large glass bead (for eye)
small white pebbles
iridescent white glass nuggets
brown, buff and black pebbles
green and white glass sea
  beans (or glass nuggets)
gold mosaic tile

equipment

plastic or metal tray, approx.
  45 x 36cm (18 x 14in)
wire cutters
rubber gloves
bucket
trowel
skewer or pointed stick
tile cutter

1 Cut a piece of chicken wire to fit inside the tray. Place it in the tray. (If you are using a metal tray, first line with kitchen foil, allowing it to overlap the tray at all four sides.)

2 Wearing rubber gloves, mix the cement (see basic techniques, pages 110–111). Carefully pour the cement into the tray, on top of the chicken wire.

3 Push the cement into all the corners of the tray. Push the chicken wire flat to prevent it rising to the surface. Tap the side of the tray to encourage air bubbles to rise and the mixture to level. Make the cement about 4cm (1½in) deep. Smooth with a trowel. Water will appear on the surface. If it is very wet, dry off slightly with a paper towel.

4 Using the template (*see* page 114), cut out a paper fish and place it diagonally in the tray.

5 Using flat glass discs (or beads), pick out the outline of the fish's body, but not the tail. Make sure the discs are pushed in to at least half their diameter otherwise they will come out later.

6 Using a tile cutter, cut strips of slate to fit around the fish's tail. The pieces should not be too narrow: no less than 2.5cm (1in).

7 Place the slate strips edge down in the cement to mark out the tail area. This area will be filled in with slate to give a different texture to the rest of the fish.

8 Remove the paper template and push in three pieces of slate to form a fin. Put the large glass bead in the centre of the head area to form an eye and draw the head section using the skewer or pointed stick. Draw wiggly lines in the cement running in the same direction as the fish.

9 Push the white pebbles into the head following the drawn line, being careful to keep them in neat rows. Fill the entire head in this way. Press all the pebbles in lengthways, to at least half their depth or 1.5cm (⅝in) (see basic techniques, pages 110–111).

◀ **10** Press the iridescent white glass nuggets into the drawn lines. These lines will help to add movement and sparkle to your finished design.

◀ **11** In between the bands of nuggets press the other stones and pebbles, starting on the outside of the fish and following the contours of its body. It is important to keep the shades in separate bands rather than mixing them all together. At this stage, also fill the tail area with strips of slate, as shown.

▶12 To fill in the fish, start by dividing it into four sections using vertical rows of white pebbles. Next, starting from the tail and working in rows across the body, push in rows of green glass sea beans into the cement, angling them slightly to give the impression of scales. In the next sections, vary the pattern with alternate rows of green and white. End with green for the tail.

◀13 Cut the gold mosaic tile into small strips using a tile cutter and decorate around the eye. Allow to dry for at least two days before removing from the tray. The fish can be cleaned with a proprietary cement cleaner.

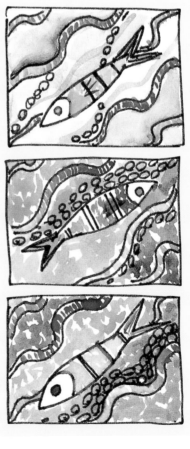

further inspiration...

upstream 19

silver fish

A simple project with lovely results. All the patterns and pebbles are pressed into a slab of potter's clay. The slab is then made into a simple mould and filled with plaster of Paris. Once set, the plaque is painted and gilded using Dutch metal leaf. It is so quick and easy to make plaques like this that you could make a variety – with different patterns – as gifts.

You can use many different pebbles. Here, black and white ones add boldness and texture to the design. Bear in mind, though, that on the finished plaque everything is reversed: thus the more you push something into the clay the more it will protrude from the plaster plaque.

silver fish 21

silver fish steps

materials

potter's clay
clingfilm
thick card
small black and white pebbles
gold glass nuggets
plaster of Paris
D-ring hook
shiny paper
white tissue paper
water-based paints
size (*see materials, page* 104)
Dutch metal sheet in
 gold and silver
fine glasspaper (optional)
spirit-based clear varnish
water-based varnish (optional)

equipment

rolling pin
craft knife
ruler
pencil
bucket
stirring stick
scissors

◀ Cover a large ball of clay with clingfilm and roll out to a thickness of 2cm (¾in). Cut to make a square approximately 26 × 26cm (10 × 10in).

2▶ Using the templates (see page 115), cut out the shapes in thick card. You will need a fish, a large square, a small square and a triangle.

3◀ With the clingfilm still in place carefully press the shapes into the clay. Start with the outside triangles and make sure the shape is deep enough to be clear. Next, press in the central square, making sure there is an even border around it. Push in the fish on top of this. The middle fish must be reversed so that it is pointing in the opposite direction to the other two. Press the small squares down each side.

4 Remove the clingfilm and, using the edge of a piece of stiff card, make background patterns around the fish. A gentle rolling motion works best. Apply the same lined pattern to the raised triangles nearest the fish. Decorate the borders of the main rectangle with large dots made with the end of a pencil (but do not push in too deeply).

5 Apply the pebbles. Mark out a border around the central area in small white pebbles and then make a double border down each side. Press the black pebbles into the undecorated triangles. Keep the pebbles in tight, neat rows and remember the deeper you push in the stones the more they will protrude in the finished piece. Finally, put the gold nuggets in place, domed side down.

6 Roll out four clay strips, 5cm (2in) wide by 2cm (¾in) thick, and of sufficient length to go all round the outside of the clay slab. Carefully attach the strips vertically around each side, to make the mould. (A little water helps the surfaces to stick.) Press hard to seal the joints.

7 Mix the plaster (see basic techniques, page 112) and pour slowly into the mould. Do not fill right to the top: allow about 1cm (½in) between the surface of the plaster and the top of the walls of the mould. The plaster should be about 2–2.5cm (¾–1in) deep. Gently tap the table next to the mould to encourage air bubbles to rise. While the plaster is still wet, push the D-ring hook into the centre of it, a third of the way from the top. Allow the plaster to harden for 2–3 hours. (During this time the plaster becomes very warm, which is quite normal.)

silver fish 23

◀8 Very gently peel the clay off the plaster. Remove any residual clay with water and a soft brush. Do not scrub too hard. Then allow the plaster to dry until it becomes harder, whiter and lighter. Allow the plaque to dry in a warm place for at least several days. (The speed of drying will depend on the room temperature.)

◀9 To decorate the fish, first tear shiny paper into thin strips and glue it along the bodies. Next, apply a covering of white tissue paper to the whole fish. When gilded, this will give an interesting texture that will contrast with the rest of the plaque.

◀10 Paint the background using any water-based paints. This plaque has turquoise for the fishes' background, a frame of bright blue and finally a dark green for the outside border.

24 simple designs

▶ Using size, paint the dots, the triangles and the fish (do not paint over the fish's blue stripes) and allow to dry for 20 minutes. (Size can be left longer as it remains tacky indefinitely.) Cut fish and triangle shapes out of the Dutch metal sheet and carefully apply it, face down. The metal will come away from its backing sheet on contact with the size. The dots can be applied from a single sheet. Don't worry if you miss a bit: you can easily fill in with more metal.

▲12 To give a softer metallic effect you can lightly sand the metal using a fine glasspaper. Here the fish were sanded, but the other gold was left solid. Finally, apply a coat of clear varnish (spirit-based) to the gold and silver to prevent tarnishing. You can also seal the rest of the frame with a water-based varnish if required.

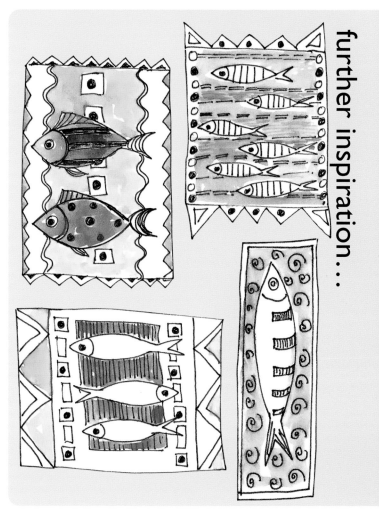

further inspiration...

silver fish 25

heart mirror

This fabulous mirror frame is ideal for those who have sneaked the odd beautiful pebble into their pockets whilst strolling along a beach, or who were seduced by tiny expensive bags of pebbles in designer shops but didn't have enough for a large pebble project.

The frame is made from plaster by first making a mould of potter's clay. When set, the plaster is painted and gilded. The differently hued pebbles add texture and interest. Don't be afraid to add more pebbles to the frame if you are lucky enough to have some beauties!

heart mirror steps

materials

potter's clay
clingfilm
thick card
mirror 8 x 11cm (3¼ x 4½in)
tiny black pebbles
small white pebbles
glass nuggets
6 'special' pebbles
2 metal screw eyes
wooden skewer
plaster of Paris
water-based paint
matt water-based varnish
size (*see materials, page 104*)
Dutch metal sheet in gold
  and silver
very fine sandpaper
spirit-based gloss varnish
3 large blue beads
picture wire

equipment

rolling pin
craft knife
ruler
skewer or pointed stick
bowl for mixing plaster
stirring stick
scissors

⚠ Cover a large ball of clay with clingfilm and roll out to a thickness of 2cm (¾in). Using the templates (*see page 116*), cut out the shapes in thick card.

◀2 Put the largest shape on the rolled-out clay and draw around it using a craft knife. Remove the template and cut the shape out. Remove the clingfilm. Keep the remainder of the rolled-out clay for later.

▶3 Put the largest rectangle in the middle of the clay shape, making sure there is an even border around it. Cut around it and remove the central piece of clay. Cover this small piece of clay in a larger sheet of clingfilm and roll out to 1cm (⅜in) thick (ie half its original thickness). Now cut the same sized rectangle out of this using the same rectangle template. Re-insert this new, thinner piece in the original gap.

4 Place the mirror on a piece of rolled-out clay and cut around it. Remove the mirror and place the clay in the centre of the large rectangle in the frame. Be careful you don't distort the shape. Cover the whole thing with clingfilm.

5 Mark out the pattern, starting with two horizontal lines on each side. Next, make simple zigzags using a small piece of card to make the marks. Push the smallest card rectangle into the top centre of the frame. Then push the heart shape into the clay. Using a skewer or pointed stick, make little dots around the heart at the top, down the sides and around the central section of the frame.

6 Remove the clingfilm. Place a 'frame' of tiny black pebbles around the top motif. Alternating one white stone and two glass nuggets, make a pattern down each side of the central area. A row of the special pebbles at the top and at the bottom completes the effect. All the stones should be pressed halfway in the clay.

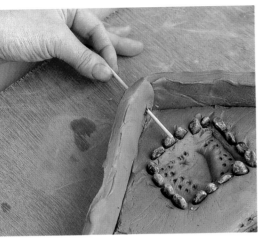

7 Roll out four clay strips 5cm (2in) wide by 2cm (¾in) thick, and of sufficient length to go all round the outside of the frame. Carefully attach the strips vertically around each side, to make the mould. (A little water helps the surfaces to stick.) Press hard to seal the joints. Take a wooden skewer and push it through the clay wall at the top of the frame. Allow about 8cm (3in) to jut out. Finally put the mirror face down in the centre.

8 Mix the plaster (see basic techniques, page 112) and pour slowly into the mould. Do not fill right to the top: allow about 1cm (½in) between the surface of the plaster and the top of the walls of the mould. The plaster should be about 2–2.5cm (¾–1in) deep. Gently tap the table next to the mould to encourage air bubbles to rise.

While the plaster is still wet, insert two metal screw eyes three-quarters of the way up the frame and 10cm (4in) apart. Allow the plaster to harden for 2–3 hours. (During this time the plaster becomes very warm, which is quite normal.)

9 Very gently peel the clay off the plaster. Remove any residual clay with water and a soft brush. Do not scrub too hard. Then allow it to dry until the plaster becomes harder, whiter and lighter. (The speed of drying will depend on the room temperature.) If the edges are a little bumpy they can be carefully sanded flat.

10 Using water-based paint, paint the inner edge turquoise, the stone section pale orange and the rest a darker shade of orange. Allow to dry, and varnish with a matt water-based varnish.

▶ Apply size to the triangles, hearts and spots and the top heart motif. Allow to dry for at least 20 minutes. Meanwhile, cut out four hearts in gold, and twelve triangles and a rectangle in silver. Spots do not need to be cut out: simply cut long strips.

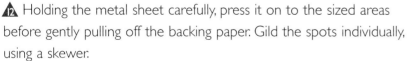

12 Holding the metal sheet carefully, press it on to the sized areas before gently pulling off the backing paper. Gild the spots individually, using a skewer.

Leave the gold solid. The silver should be lightly sanded using very fine glasspaper and given a wash of diluted orange paint. This gives the metal a 'softer' feel. Allow to dry.

Varnish all the gilded areas with a spirit-based gloss varnish. Glue three large blue beads on the wooden spike, trimming off any excess wood. Connect the two screw eyes at the back with picture wire. Hang on a wall, stand back and admire.

further inspiration...

heart mirror 31

pure pebbles

This project uses plastic resin to enhance the beauty of pebbles, copper and glass. The effect is to display their tone and shape, revealing all the markings and details, and making the glass nuggets look like jewels.

The result can be enjoyed just as a decorative object, or it could be used for practical purposes. For example, three would make a delightful splash-back above a washbasin. Alternatively, they could be hung in front of a window to allow the sunlight to shine through and highlight the glass nuggets.

materials

resin (with catalyst)
copper sheet (shim)
blue and green glass nuggets
light blue glass sea beans
6 beautiful pebbles

equipment

plastic container,
  approx. 23 x 20cm (9 x 8in)
ruler
measuring jug
rubber gloves
mask
thick card
scissors
pencil
paper
wooden stick

A Pour water into the plastic container to a depth of 1cm (½in), using a ruler to check the level.

2 Pour the water into a measuring jug to check the amount. Take a note of the figure. Throw away the water.

3 Halve the above figure and mix this amount of liquid resin and catalyst (hardener), following the manufacturer's instructions. Make sure you wear rubber gloves and a mask, and work in a well ventilated room, or preferably outside. Pour the resin solution into the plastic container and allow it to set until it is solid but still sticky (this will take approximately 2 hours, depending on the room temperature).

4 Using the template (see page 117), cut out the spiral shape in thick card. Use the card shape to draw the spiral on the copper sheet. Using scissors, cut out the copper spiral.

5 Pressing hard with a pencil, draw horizontal lines on the spiral to give an interesting pattern and texture.

6 Arrange the spiral, glass nuggets and pebbles in a pattern on a piece of paper the same size as the plastic container. This will make it easier to transfer them to the resin. Very carefully place the spiral on the resin which will still be sticky. Put the rest of the pebbles and glass nuggets around it.

7 Mix the same quantity of resin again and very slowly pour it over the stones. Use a wooden stick to push any pebbles back into position.

8 Allow the resin to dry thoroughly before removing the resin from the plastic container. (The speed of drying will depend on the room temperature and the amount of catalyst added. See the manufacturer's instructions.) If there are any fingerprints or scratches on the surface they can be removed with wet and dry abrasive paper and button polish.

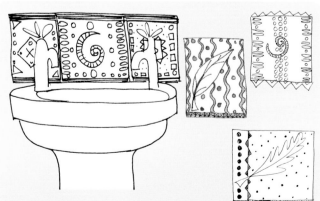

further inspiration…

pure pebbles 35

intermediate designs

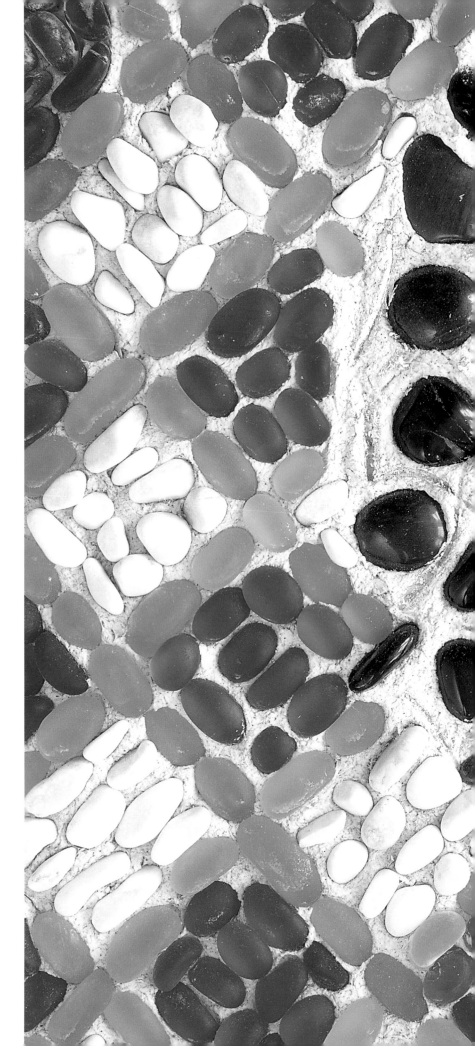

patchwork

Based on the idea of a patchwork quilt, this design is made by combining small individual blocks of pebble mosaic made in disposable foil trays. The variety of small blocks is then assembled – like patchwork – into a larger area.

This is a delightful project for children at home or in the classroom as everyone can make their own small design to be combined into a larger area. Children could provide their own contributions in the form of a treasured stone or bead.

The resulting patchwork can be used in several ways. This one has been made into a charming outdoor table, setting it on an old, iron sewing-machine base. It would look equally striking as part of a garden design, patio decoration, doorstep or hearth.

patchwork steps

materials

disposable foil food trays,
  approx. 20 x 10 x 4.5cm
  (8 x 4 x 1¾in)
cement and coarse sand (or
  ready-mixed sand and cement)
mosaic tiles
pebbles
glass nuggets
glass sea beans
beads
chicken wire
wood or MDF board
  (size depends on quilt size)
4 pieces of wood, 7 x 2cm
  (2¾ x ¾in): length depends
  on board size
screws
soft paintbrush
tile adhesive (optional)
external water-based paint
  (optional)

equipment

bucket
trowel
saw
screwdriver

⚠ Wearing rubber gloves, mix the cement (see basic techniques, pages 110–111). The amount depends on how many trays you are going to fill. If in doubt, work in small batches. Fill a foil tray approximately half full. Divide the tray in half with a drawn line or a row of mosaic tiles.

2 Fill in each half using a variety of patterns. Push the materials in vertically. Don't be afraid to experiment: for example, one particularly beautiful pebble could form the middle of a simple flower, or a sparkly bead will make a fish's eye. Carefully fill in the backgrounds to the main designs.

3 For the best effects make sure the two halves of each tray are different, to make two different 'patches'. This project uses 15 trays, giving 30 different patches.

◀ 4 Allow to dry for several days before removing from the metal trays. The size of the finished piece will be determined by the number of blocks you have made. Experiment with blocks in different positions to form a variety of patterns. Lay them out before you start the next stage.

5 ▶ Allow a border of at least 5cm (2in) around the outside of the positioned blocks. Cut a piece of blockboard, MDF, or similar to fit. Also cut two pieces of 7 × 2cm (2¾ × ¾in) wood the same length as the longer side. Cut another two pieces of wood to fit along the other two sides, between the two longer pieces. Join the four sides together and then screw them to the base board.

6 Cut a piece of chicken wire to fit inside the frame. Mix up sufficient cement to make a layer 2cm (¾in) thick inside the frame. Wearing gloves, pour this into the frame, lifting the chicken wire slightly so it is surrounded by cement.

◀ 7 Position the blocks closely together in the frame, on top of the cement. Press down firmly. Make sure there is a border around the outside of the design. Mix a small quantity of cement and use this to fill the gaps, ignoring the outside border.

8 Use a soft brush to make clean, tidy joints. Cement shrinks slightly so these joints should be slightly proud.

9 Fill in the border around the blocks with cement.

10 Fill in the outer border with neat bands of white pebbles, packing them closely together. Allow to dry for several days before unscrewing the frame.

If the sides are on show, either decorate with further pebbles or mosaic tiles, using tile adhesive to stick them down, or paint the sides with external water-based paint.

further inspiration...

daisy hearth

A stylish hearth design that is deceptively simple, relying on a few really beautiful pebbles. The subtle changes from cream through ochre to buff are emphasized by the pristine white background bordered in black. Based on pretty country flowers, this stunning design would look equally at home in a rustic country cottage or a contemporary city loft. It is a purely decorative device and not suitable for a hearth used with an open fire.

As with many designs in this book, be prepared to adapt the designs to the pebbles you have available. If you have a large collection of small beautiful pebbles, try a different shaped flower with lots of petals. No round pebbles? Use a copper disc, the end of a flowerpot, or another contrasting material.

daisy hearth steps

materials

wood for surround
nails
wood glue
strong plastic tape (optional)
wooden board for laying out
  design, same size as hearth
  area
cement and coarse sand (or
  ready-mixed sand and cement)
small white pebbles
medium black pebbles
small brown/buff pebbles
2 large round pebbles,
  preferably dark
medium cream pebbles
'special' medium pebbles
spirit-based gloss varnish

equipment

saw
hammer
scissors
rubber gloves
bucket
trowel
small artist's brush

▲ Measure the hearth area and make a wooden surround at least 3cm (1¼in) high. Pine is ideal and can be stained and varnished to match the room. Nail and glue into place. If you have any gaps between floorboards seal them using a strong plastic tape.

▲ On a board the same size as the hearth and using the templates (see page 118), lay out the design (not the background). This will allow you to make decisions about hue and shape.

Brown and buff pebbles have been used for the leaves and smooth cream pebbles for the stems. (In this design it is extremely important that the pebbles are an even size and shape.) The real beauties were kept for the flowers.

3 Wearing rubber gloves, mix the cement (see techniques, pages 110–111). Put it into the hearth surround and use a float or trowel to smooth the surface. The surface of the cement should be about 5mm (¼in) below the top edge of the wood.

4 Either draw the approximate position of the flowers and leaves on the cement or draw around a paper pattern to get the position of the design (this will be approximate, as it will depend on the pebbles available).

5 Carefully transfer the design to the hearth area, starting with the centre of a flower (try to get a large round pebble for this) and working outwards forming concentric circles of round white pebbles to represent stamens. Push the pebbles in firmly.

6 It is important that the patterns are clear and neat in this project, with only gradual changes in shade and tone, and pebbles set in various directions to emphasize the patterns.

7 Place the cream pebbles in position to make stems. Make the leaves by starting with the leaf's outside edge and working inwards in tight linear rows.

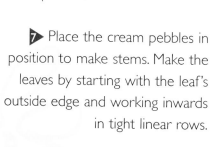

8 Place a single row of black pebbles inside the wooden surround to form a frame. A row of fancy pebbles has been used to make the demarcation line between the hearth and fire. Now fill in the background with white pebbles. It is extremely useful to have more than one pair of hands doing this as the cement can begin to dry quite quickly. The pebbles will not stick if the cement is too dry.

9 To enhance the shades of the pebbles, varnish the darker ones.

further inspiration....

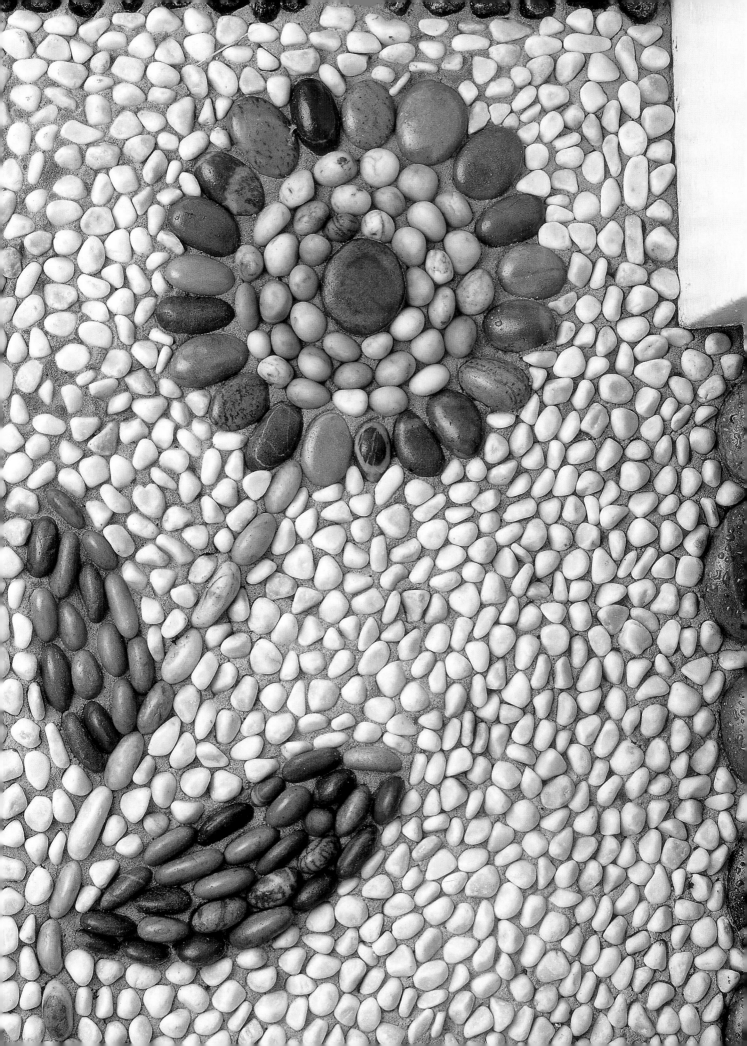

mosaic arrival

A front doorstep is the perfect place for a pebble mosaic, making a real feature. Even the most ordinary entrance will be transformed into something special with the addition of pebble shapes and patterns. When designing for small areas, remember to keep the shapes and patterns simple and distinctive to emphasize the shades and texture.

This project is made in four sections of the same size, in wooden frames, indoors, then the four slabs are assembled *in situ.* The border and background are filled in afterwards (particularly helpful when the shape is awkward). This method of working is wonderfully flexible, allowing mosaics to be made inside in comfort. Both large and small projects can be made this way.

mosaic arrival

steps

materials

wooden board, 15–18mm
   (⅝–¾in) thick, approx. one
   quarter the size of the step
   area (see step 1)
4 strips wood, 7 x 2cm
   (2¾ x ¾in) to fit around board
screws
cement and coarse sand (or
   ready-mixed sand and cement)
pencil
18 shiny black pebbles
30 smooth white pebbles
dark green glass nuggets,
   30 per petal
light green iridescent glass
   nuggets, 30 per petal
small white pebbles
dark green pebbles
wooden batten for front of
   the step (see step 11)
masonry nails

equipment

tape measure
saw
screwdriver
wire cutters
rubber gloves
bucket
trowel
spirit level
soft paintbrush

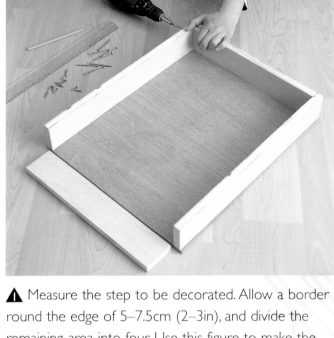

▲ Measure the step to be decorated. Allow a border round the edge of 5–7.5cm (2–3in), and divide the remaining area into four. Use this figure to make the wooden frame, then cut the wooden board to size and screw together the four pieces of wood so they fit around the board.

◄2 Attach the board to the strips using screws. You can make more than one frame or use the same one four times.

◄3 Cut a piece of chicken wire to fit the frame and place inside. Wearing rubber gloves, mix the cement (see basic techniques, pages 110–111). Pour it into the frame, lifting the chicken wire slightly so it is surrounded by cement. Use a trowel to smooth the surface.

4 Working diagonally from corner to corner press in two rows of white pebbles. (Drawing a line in the cement will keep the lines straight.)

5 Measure 15cm (6in) down each of two adjoining sides and draw another diagonal straight line in the cement. Press in two more rows of white pebbles. Draw the zigzag patterns using a pencil and then push in a single row of white pebbles along these lines.

6 Using the template (see page 119), draw the flower centre and three petals radiating from it. Fill in first with approximately four or five black shiny pebbles, then a double row of white smooth pebbles (approximately seven), then a double row of small white pebbles. Next, make the petals using the glass nuggets in linear patterns radiating from the centre. Alternate the shades of the nuggets for each petal.

mosaic arrival 53

7 ► Make the heart in the opposite corner. Fill in with white pebbles.

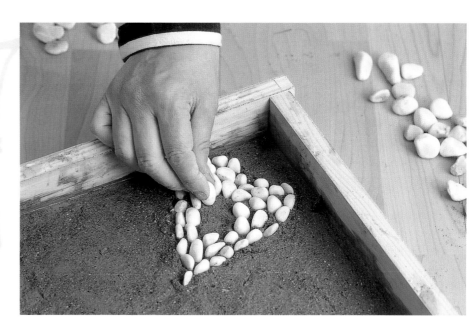

8 ◄ Fill in all the remaining background using green pebbles. Make two identical slabs and then – THIS IS VERY IMPORTANT – turn all the templates over and make two more slabs in a mirror image of the others. (This means all four will fit together.) Allow all the slabs to dry for several days before unscrewing the frame.

9 ► Find the centre of the front doorstep (houses and steps are rarely completely square). Draw a line and place the slabs, two either side, on the step, so that the flower motif and diagonal patterns meet up.

◀10 Mix up some more cement. Put large blobs of cement under each slab and press firmly into position using a spirit level to check they are all level and the same height.

▶11 Attach a wooden batten the same thickness as the slabs to the front of the step, and nail into position using masonry nails. Mix sufficient cement to fill in around the slabs, to just below their surface level. Using a small damp brush fill in the small gaps between the slabs.

◀12 If you have an awkwardly shaped step area add extra decoration. Here, a heart has been added to echo the motif in the slabs.

◀ **3** Using the same green stones as the slabs' background, fill in the cemented area. Allow the step to dry for five days before walking on it.

further inspiration…

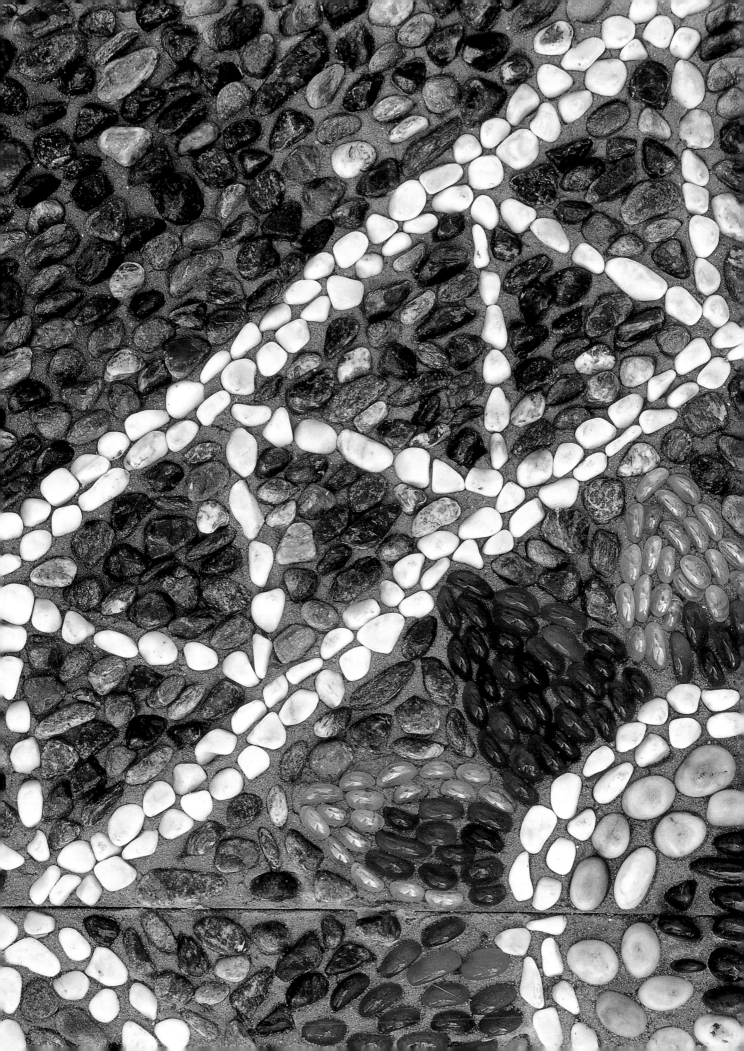

topiary tree

Working in a base of papier mâché rather than cement gives pebbles a different dimension. Because it dries much more slowly than cement, a complicated piece of work can be made over several days. Just keep the board covered in clingfilm to prevent it drying out. Papier mâché is also cleaner and more flexible than cement.

Based on topiary and formal gardens, this project is ideal for a conservatory or garden room. The most difficult part is placing the large pebbles to give an impression of leaves. The trick is to stand well back and look at the pattern with half-closed eyes.

Papier mâché is not really suitable for the outside. However, if you really want it in the garden, several coats of yacht varnish will greatly prolong its life.

topiary tree 59

materials

5 litres (½ bucketful)
  papier-mâché pulp (see basic
  techniques, page 113)
large blockboard or MDF,
  approx 90 x 60 x 1.5cm
  (36 x 24 x ⅝in)
PVA glue
thick card
medium brown/buff pebbles
strip of slate, approx 25 x 3cm
  (10 x 1¼in)
large polished black pebbles
  (long, leaf-shaped ones are best)
turquoise glass sea beans
blue glass sea beans
small black pebbles
small white pebbles
Dutch metal sheet in silver
size (see materials, page 104)
spirit-based gloss varnish

equipment

liquidizer
saucepan
rolling pin
plastic spreader or corraflute
scissors
Ruler or piece of wood
  1m (39in) long
artist's brushes

1 Prepare the papier-mâché pulp. Using the plastic spreader or corraflute, spread a thin layer of PVA glue on the wooden board.

Firmly squash a layer of papier-mâché pulp on the board. It is not necessary to go right to the edges. Cover the pulp with clingfilm.

2 Using a rolling pin, roll the pulp evenly. Remove the excess pulp that falls off the edges of the board. The finished pulp should be approximately 1cm (½in) thick.

3 Remove the clingfilm. Use a plastic spreader or piece of corraflute to smooth the pulp and tidy the edges. If any pulp leaves the surface just smooth it down again.

4 Re-cover the pulp with clingfilm and, using the edge of a ruler to press a line into the pulp, make a horizontal line 7cm (2¾in) from the bottom of the board. Along this line make small marks every 8cm (3in). Repeat the 8cm (3in) measurements along the top and down both sides.

Taking the ruler or piece of wood, join the bottom left corner with the top right corner using the edge to press a line into the pulp. Continue along the top, joining a mark at the top with one on the side.

Continue until the board (except for the bottom 7cm) is covered with evenly spaced diagonal lines. Now go the other way by joining the marks at the top left with the bottom right. Repeat as before to make a trellis pattern.

5 Leaving the clingfilm in place, measure the centre of the horizontal line on the board. Using the template (see page 120), cut out a flowerpot shape in thick card. Press this firmly into the pulp, on top of the clingfilm, in the centre of the board, with the bottom just below the horizontal line.

6 Remove the clingfilm. Arrange the brown pebbles on the flowerpot area in neat rows, putting similar shades of brown next to each other. Glue them in place and push down firmly.

7 Glue the slate strip into position, protruding vertically from the middle of the pot. Using the template (see page 120), cut out the circle shape. Cover the area at the top of the slate with clingfilm to prevent sticking. Draw around the template. Remove the clingfilm and use the plastic spreader to remove the trellis marks from inside the circle, leaving a smooth round shape.

topiary tree 61

8▷ Start placing the shiny black pebbles into the pulp, starting with the largest ones. Space the pebbles evenly, pointing them in different directions to represent the way in which leaves grow

9▷ Continue to fill in the tree. Use smaller pebbles to make the outside leaves. These should break out of the drawn circle. (If you find this difficult, put the pebbles on a piece of paper first to work out the pattern.) Glue into position, pressing firmly into the pulp.

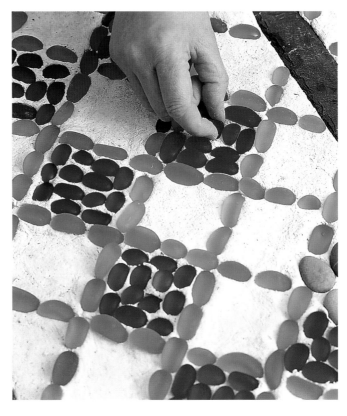

10▷ Mark the lines of the trellis using turquoise glass sea beans. Glue them down lengthways along all the diagonal lines. Press them in firmly.

11◁ Start to fill in the trellis using blue glass sea beans. Make tight, neat patterns and glue into place. Fill in every alternate square. Press in firmly.

62 intermediate designs

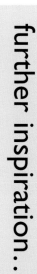

13 Cover the leaf area in clingfilm. Using a strip of card, bent in the middle, press into the pulp between the black stones to indicate branches. Don't put in too many lines.

Allow the mosaic to dry until completely hard. (The speed of drying will depend on the room temperature, but will take up to two weeks.)

Once the papier mâché is dry, paint the 'branches' with metal size and gild in silver. Varnish all the gilded areas with a spirit-based gloss varnish to prevent tarnishing.

12 Use the small black pebbles to fill in the ground level. The black floor will enhance the black leaves. The white pebbles should now be pressed into place in the rest of the trellis to give an exciting textural contrast.

further inspiration…

elaborate designs

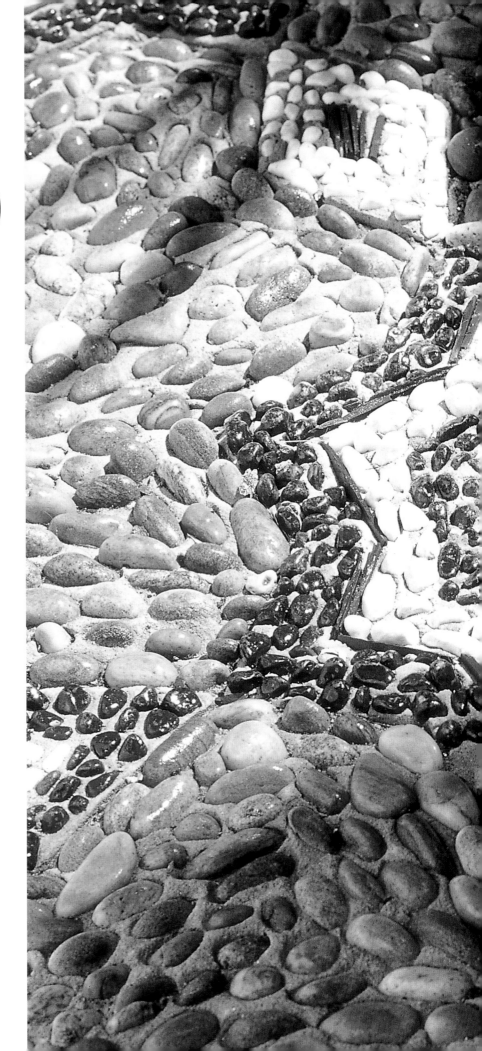

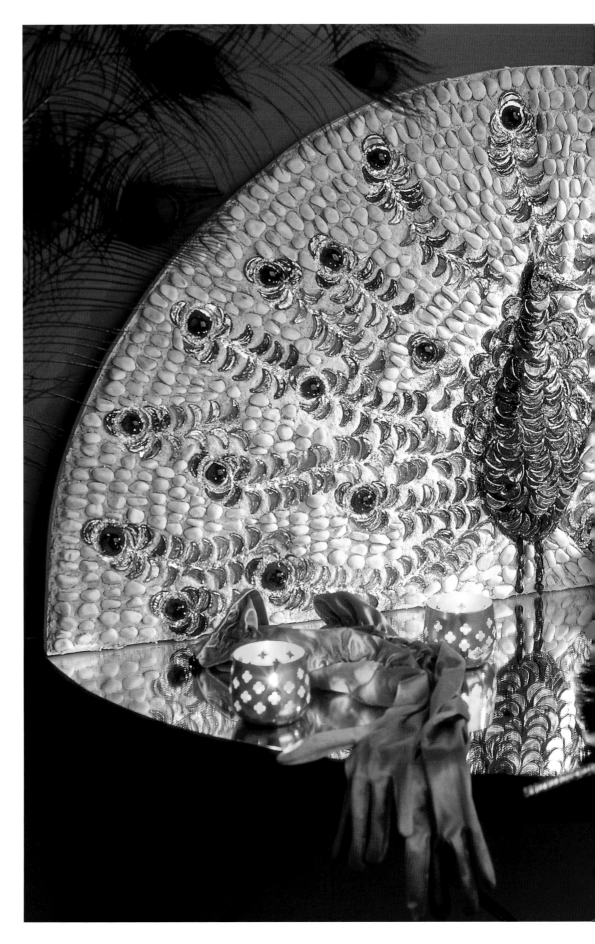

peacock fan

Many pebble mosaics rely on the pattern of the pebbles as much as on the variety of hues, and this project is a prime example. Based on a stylized peacock and reminiscent of late-Victorian motifs, the real dynamism comes from the colour and movement of the glass shapes that make up the feathers. Before making your design, lay out the peacock on a piece of board and play around with the feathers. See how a curved line gives a very different feel to a straight one. Try spacing out the glass 'moons' to see the effect.

This beautiful piece has been designed as a table back, but would look equally striking as a picture or the top of a hallway mirror. It could also be made in cement for the garden.

peacock fan steps

materials

wooden blockboard or MDF, approx
  1.5cm (⅝in) thick (see templates, page 121)
5 litres (½ bucketful) papier-mâché pulp
  (see basic techniques, page 113)
PVA glue
small white pebbles
approx 10 tiny black pebbles
iridescent dark blue moons (approx. 56)
iridescent turquoise blue moons (approx. 230)
iridescent green moons (approx. 230)
12 x 3cm (1¼in) turquoise glass pendants
  (donuts)
12 x 3cm (1¼in) blue flat glass
  pendants (donuts)
24 dark blue glass nuggets
water-based paints
size (see materials, page 114)
Dutch metal sheet in
  gold and silver
glasspaper (optional)
gold paint
jewellery wire
36 small tubular beads
16 small beads various colours
spirit-based gloss varnish

equipment

pencil
string
large nail
jigsaw or saw
glasspaper
liquidizer
saucepan
rolling pin
plastic spreader or corraflute
skewer or pointed stick
artist's brushes

▲ Using the template (see page 121), draw the semicircle on the wooden board. (Alternatively, decide the length and height of the peacock and draw the base line of the semicircle. Divide in half and hammer a long nail into the middle point of the base. Attach a piece of string, stretch this to one side from the middle and tie to a pencil. Keeping the string taut, draw the semicircle.) Cut out with a jigsaw. Sand down any rough edges.

  Cover the board in a thin film of PVA glue. Firmly squash a layer of papier-mâché pulp on the board. It is not necessary to go right to the edges. Cover the pulp with clingfilm.

2 Using a rolling pin, roll the pulp evenly. Remove the excess pulp that falls off the edges of the board. The finished pulp should be approximately 1cm (½in) thick. Remove the clingfilm. Use a plastic spreader or piece of corraflute to smooth the pulp and tidy the edges.

3 Using the template (see page 121), cut out the body and draw around it in the middle of the board using a skewer or pointed stick.

Next draw the feathers in the pulp (one line is sufficient). Feel free to add extra feathers if you wish.

4 Take a large piece of extra pulp and roll it in your hands to make a fattish sausage shape approximately the same size as the peacock's body. Apply a little glue to the area and press the body into position, flattening it in the process.

Add a thinner sausage shape for the neck, a small ball for the head and a cone shape for the beak. Flatten and glue into place as before. Using the plastic spreader, smooth the body thoroughly. Don't be tempted to wet the pulp.

5 Taking the dark blue glass moon shapes, work down each side of the body gluing them into place. Note the direction of the moons. These need to represent layered feathers so it is very important to have them lying the same way as in the photo. Do not fill in the head. Once complete, gently press all the moons into the pulp.

Now make the tail base. This runs down each side of the body (see step 6). Start one third of the way up, on the left-hand side. Press a row of seven green moons joined by the points (the longer curved side is vertical and pointing away from the body). In between the gaps put four more moons to make a scale-like pattern. Repeat on the other side.

7 Fill in all of the background using small white pebbles. Press them in neat, tight linear patterns.

6 Next, work on the tail feathers. Work along each one, evenly spacing the moons. End each tail feather with a contrasting colour (green for turquoise feathers and vice versa), using five moons surrounding one of the large pendants (donuts). Glue a dark blue glass nugget on the disc. Vary the feather colours by making the 'eye' in the opposite colour.

8 Make the peacock's legs from two rows of small black pebbles. Fill in any remaining gaps with white pebbles.

9 Allow the mosaic to dry until completely hard. (The speed of drying will depend on the room temperature, but will take up to two weeks.)

When dry, paint the head and the body a light shade of blue, using water-based paint.

10 Paint metal size in the tail-base area between the green moons, around the 'eye' areas and along the middle of the feathers.

11 Cut strips of Dutch metal and press gold around the 'eyes' and silver down the middle of the feathers.

12 Continue to fill in with gold, gently rubbing it into the tail-base area to give a 'broken' effect. This can be made more pronounced by using glasspaper to 'soften' the gold.

13 Paint the head, using washes of blue, turquoise and green water-based paint. Finish with a coat of very dilute gold paint. Paint the eye and the beak black (or use a felt-tipped pen). Outline the eye in a little gold and add decorative dots.

peacock fan 71

14 Cut eight pieces of wire, about 5cm (2in) long. Thread the beads on to the wire, turning it over at one end to prevent the beads from falling off. Glue to the top of the head. Varnish the head, beak and legs.

further inspiration...

fountain swirl

A copper fish spouts water from its tail on to a blue and turquoise mosaic 'pool' which is surrounded by a classically inspired black and white design. The effect is stunning and would make a wonderful centrepiece to any garden.

This project looks really complicated, but it is easier to make than it seems. The water feature, powered by a small pump, is assembled on a plastic bin or tub. The pump sits inside the tub with a plastic flowerpot over it.

The 'inner pool' mosaic (made in blue and turquoise) rests on the upturned flowerpot. There is a small gap between the inner pool and the black and white mosaic. Water passes from the pump up through the fish, and dribbles back down to the pump again though the gap between the mosaics.

copper fish

materials

chicken wire, 56 x 34cm
  (22 x 13½in)
copper sheet (shim)
thin copper wire
waterproof glue
2 x 3cm (1¼in) blue glass
  pendants (donuts)

equipment

wire cutters
ballpoint pen
scissors
hammer
nail

1 Take the piece of chicken wire and make a long cylindrical shape approximately 11cm (4⅓in) in diameter, allowing the wire to overlap. Push the cut ends of the wire through the sides of the cylinder and bend over so it stays in place. Flatten to approximately 4cm (1½in) wide. Squeeze together one end to form a rounded shape.

2 At the other end, in the middle of the flat side, make a cut of about 9cm (3½in) through the two layers of wire. Push these two sections apart (they will form the two tail fins) and squeeze the top and bottom together turning the ends of each to make points. Make all the sharp ends bend in.

3 Refine the shape by squeezing very firmly just in front of the tail. The wire will compress if even pressure is exerted. Repeat at the head so it also tapers.

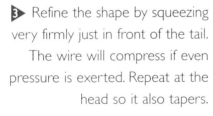

◀ Using the templates (see, page 122) and copper sheet, cut out four tail shapes, scales and the head section. Using a ballpoint pen, firmly draw straight lines on the back of the copper tail pieces, and the lines on the scales.

5 Using a hammer and nail, make regular holes along the tail section edges. Place two pieces of tail together over the chicken wire structure and 'sew' together using copper wire. Repeat the other side. Starting at the tail end, apply the scales gluing one on top of the other (for extra strength these can be wired into place as well) in a scale pattern as shown.

6
Draw the decorative pattern on the head using a ballpoint pen as before (see templates, page 122).

◀ Bend the head in half (do not crease) and glue into position. Glue the blue glass eye disc in position on the fish's head.

inner pool

materials

copper pipe, 22mm (¾in) diameter, 5cm (2in) long

chicken wire

cement and coarse sand (or ready-mixed sand and cement)

chicken wire

dark blue glass nuggets

green sea beans

green glass nuggets

turquoise sea beans

turquoise glass nuggets

white pebbles

equipment

circular plastic saucer or bowl, approx 5cm (2in) deep and 5cm (2in) diameter less than the diameter of the plastic tub or bin (see page 81) pictured: plastic dustbin lid, approx. 54cm (21¼in)

clay or modelling clay

deep, square tray (optional)

wire cutters

rubber gloves

trowel

float

scissors

bucket

8 If using a dustbin lid, fill the handle section of the lid and any holes with clay or modelling clay to make a smooth, rounded base. Embed in the clay a piece of copper tube. (This must be pushed down as far as the plastic underneath otherwise there will not be a hole through the finished 'pool'.)

9 Support the saucer or lid so it is level and does not wobble around. Cut a circular piece of chicken wire to fit the lid and place inside. Wearing rubber gloves, mix the cement (see basic techniques, pages 110–111). Half fill the lid. (Lift the wire slightly so the cement surrounds it.) Use a float or trowel to smooth the surface.

10 Starting in the middle of the lid, make five concentric circles of dark blue glass nuggets.

11 Press in a circle of green sea beans (on the beans' sides), then a circle of green sea beans lengthways, two circles of green glass nuggets, and, changing direction, a further circle of turquoise sea beans. Then two circles of turquoise glass nuggets and a final circle of green sea beans (lengthways into the cement). Finish in circles of white pebbles. (Refer to the picture, left, and the picture on page 83 for guidance.)

Allow to dry, for up to three days, before removing the cement block from the lid.

outer mosaic

Two ways of working out the curve are shown so that the designs can be adapted to different or awkward sizes. There are four sections to the mosaic, so either the frame can be re-used, or more than one frame can be made.

The instructions below make four sections to fit around a circle 54cm (21¼in) in diameter.

materials

3 pieces blockboard 18mm (¾in) thick,
  50 x 50cm (20 x 20in)
2 lengths of blockboard, 30 x 6cm (12 x 2½in)
screws
2 strips ply, 1.5mm (¹⁄₁₆in) thick:
  1 approx. 69 x 4cm (27 x 1½in)
  1 approx. 41cm x 4cm (16 x 1½in)
small nails
chicken wire
cement and coarse sand (or
  ready-mixed sand and cement)
black pebbles
white pebbles

equipment

pencil
string
long nail
jigsaw
screwdriver
hammer

12 Using the template (see page 123), draw the semicircles on the wooden board. (Alternatively, use a pencil, a nail and a piece of string to mark the quarter circles. Hammer a nail into the corner of one of the boards. Attach a piece of string, then measure half the diameter of the inner pool along the string and tie a pencil at this point. Pull the string taut and draw an arc with it on the board. Untie the pencil and re-tie it a further 20cm (8in) along the string. Draw a second arc.)

Using a jigsaw, cut out the curves and use them as templates to mark the other two boards. Cut another board, leaving the third board intact.

13 Screw the three pieces together with the uncut board as a base, and attach the two side boards.

14 Attach the two strips of ply to the two inner curved edges. Tack into place.

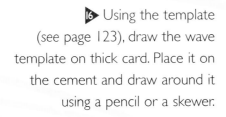

15 Cut a piece of chicken wire to fit the curved area and place inside. Mix the cement (see step 9) and pour it into the frame. Make sure the chicken wire is surrounded.

16 Using the template (see page 123), draw the wave template on thick card. Place it on the cement and draw around it using a pencil or a skewer.

◀17 Make a double row of black pebbles along the inside curve. Next, using small white pebbles, mark out the shape of the waves. Fill the waves in continuous linear patterns. Finally, fill in the rest of the background in black.

◀18 Allow to dry for up to three days before removing the block from the frame.

assembling the fountain

materials

large plastic tub, slightly wider
  than diameter of inner pool
small pump suitable for
  small fountain
plastic flowerpot to fit
  inside tub, about 5cm (2in)
  less deep
1 wine cork
copper pipe 9mm (⅜in)
  diameter x 1m (39in) long
gravel

equipment

spade
drill
hacksaw

19 Dig a hole in the ground, deep enough to accommodate the large tub with its top edge at ground level. Drill a hole just below the rim of the tub to take the pump's electrical cable. Drill another in the centre of the plastic flowerpot. Drill large holes around the rim to allow the water to flow back to the pump. Now place the pump under the upturned flowerpot and feed the cable through one of its side holes. Thread the cable through the tub hole, and attach the plug. Push the copper tubing through the centre hole of the flowerpot and attach the end inside the pot to the pump. Thread the inner pool slab on to the pipe so it sits in the large tub, resting on the flowerpot below. Drill a hole in the wine cork and thread this on the smaller copper pipe to make a watertight seal between the two pipes.

20 ► Attach the fish by firmly pushing the pipe up the middle of the fish's body so the end appears at the tail. Using a hacksaw, cut the pipe so only a little shows between the tail fins. Place the tub in the ground and fill in the soil around it. Slightly sink the four sections of the outer mosaic into the ground and surround them with gravel. Fill with water, run the pump and adjust the end of the copper pipe, reducing its size if necessary, to get the correct flow.

further inspiration…

oriental path

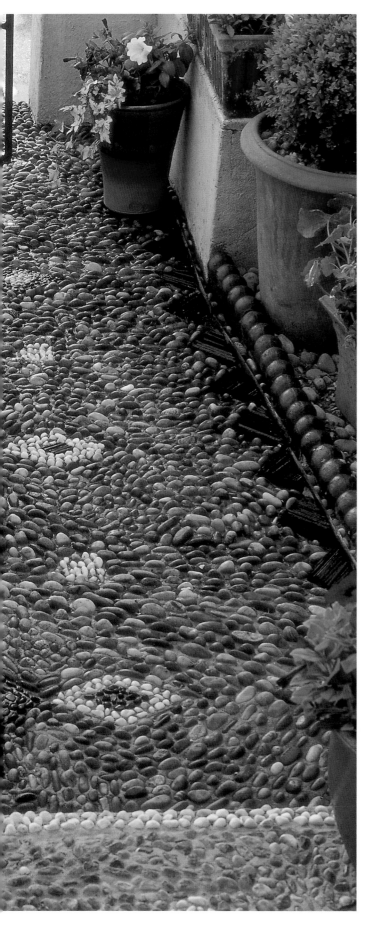

A fabulous project, guaranteed to impress your friends and neighbours. Although it looks complicated, it is just a combination of all the techniques in earlier pebble mosaics.

The geometric designs, based on oriental carpets, translate beautifully into pebble mosaics. The star and diamond motifs are made in frames indoors and the final work assembled outside. The background is then filled in using contrasting colours.

The path shown here is approximately 2.6 x 1.4m (8½ x 4½ft), but using the templates, you can adapt the design for your own path. Cut the pieces out of paper and put them into position to help you visualize the final appearance. Make sure the path is sound and level before you start.

materials

thick card

for diamond frame:

2 pieces of wood 12 x 3 x 3cm
(4¾ x 1¼ x 1¼in)

2 pieces of wood 24 x 3 x 3cm
(9½ x 1¼ x 1¼in)

wooden board 24 x 5cm x 1.5cm
(9½ x 2 x ⅝in)

cement and coarse sand (or
ready-mixed sand and cement)

small black pebbles

medium white pebbles

slate, cut into strips approximately 4cm (1½in)
wide plus thinner strips 2cm (¾in) wide

for star frame:

2 pieces of wood 32 x 6 x 3cm
(12½ x 2½ x 1¼in)

2 pieces of wood 44 x 6 x 3cm
(17½ x 2½ x 1¼in)

wooden board 48 x 48cm x 1.5cm
(19 x 19 x ⅝in) square

selection of gold mosaic tiles, red beads
and glass nuggets

34 wooden triangles with a base of 14cm
(5½in), height 7cm (2¾in) and 6cm (2½in) thick

equipment

ruler and pencil

scissors

saw or jigsaw

mitre block

screwdriver

tile or slate cutters

wire cutters

rubber gloves

trowel

bucket

spirit level

proprietary cement cleaner (optional)

**For each diamond shape you
need to make twelve finished
pieces, so it is worth making
four frames and using each
of them three times. Similarly
you need to make four star
shapes, so either make two
frames or use the same one
four times.**

▲ Using the template of the
diamond (see page 124), cut out
a pattern in thick card. Use the
pattern to mark the correct length
and angle on to the two smaller
pieces of 3cm (1¼in) square
wood. Cut using a saw and
mitre block.

3 Screw the four pieces together. Draw a pencil line running through the middle of the short pieces and on to the longer pieces. This indicates the angle of the screws. Screw the shape to the board.

2 Lay these on a board using the card pattern to get the correct angle. Put the two longer pieces of wood along the top and the bottom.

4 Wearing rubber gloves, mix up a small batch of cement (see basic techniques, pages 110–111). Fill the frame just over half full. Use a trowel to smooth the surface.

5 Make a double border of white pebbles and fill in with black ones. Make a total of four of these. In addition, you will need to make the following diamond shapes:
◆ two completely white
◆ three white with slate strips in the middle (see step 13) instead of black pebbles
◆ three black with white centres.
Allow to dry for up to two days before removing the frames.

6 Using the template of the square (see page 125), cut out a pattern in thick card. Arrange the pieces of 6 × 3cm (2½ × 1¼in) wood so they fit exactly around the square.

7 Draw lines on the wood at the centre point of each side of the square.

9 Screw the sections together using long screws. Put the star shape on the board and draw around the internal shape.

8 Line up the corners of the cardboard square with the pencil lines. Draw around the corners on the wood. Using a jigsaw or a saw, cut out these triangular sections to give a star shape when the frame is re-assembled.

◀ 10 Screw the star shape to the board with the drawn side up. This will help you put the screws in the correct place.

△ 11 Line the frame with a piece of chicken wire cut to fit. Wearing rubber gloves, mix up a small batch of cement (see basic techniques, pages 110–111). Fill the frame just over half full. Lift the chicken wire slightly so the cement completely surrounds it. Tap the frame to level the cement. Use a trowel to smooth the surface.

△ 13 Using tile or slate cutters, cut strips of slate to fit the star shape and press in until only half the width protrudes.

12 Make a border three small black pebbles wide, making sure the pebbles are pressed in firmly. Repeat using white pebbles.

14 Fill in the star with black pebbles, finishing the centre with a square of white pebbles surrounded by four glass nuggets. Allow to dry for up to two days before removing the frame. Make four of these stars, varying the centres using beads, glass nuggets or gold mosaic tiles. Try to make each one different.

15 Arrange the wooden triangles down each side of the path. Position the rest of the shapes.

16 Wearing rubber gloves, mix up a small batch of cement. Using a trowel, make a bed of cement 1cm (½in) thick and cement each shape into position. Use a long spirit level to check they are all the same height.

17 Working a section at a time, put a bed of cement around the shapes. The level should be just below the shape height. Do not be tempted to make too much cement in one go. Make it in small batches. Remember to push the pebbles in lengthways.

18 Starting at the top, work around the star so the pebbles radiate outwards. (The pebbles should be the same level as the ones embedded in the star and triangular slabs.) When you get to the halfway point between two stars, work outwards from the star beneath so the radiating patterns meet in the middle.

Completing a project of this size will inevitably mean working over several days. As a result there will be a join mark between each day's cement, but try to make it part of the pattern. Here, joins have been made equidistant between the stars. They appear as straight lines and so are not so noticeable.

Keep the design covered if wet weather is likely, otherwise your hard work will wash away!

19 Fill in the background completely. As the path is filled in it is possible to add little extra motifs. Here, a series of white small squares have been added for extra interest.

oriental path 91

▼20 Allow to dry for four to five days before walking on it. Put a series of boards or planks down if there is no other entrance. When completely dry, remove the wooden triangles and half fill the resulting spaces with cement.

▲21 Cut strips of slate to fit and, laying them in one direction, push them in firmly. They should fit tightly together. For the next triangle insert the slate in the opposite direction and so on, alternating the slates' direction in the triangles. Allow to dry. Stick back any loose pebbles with external tile adhesive. Once the path is completely dry, remove any cement residue with proprietary cement cleaner.

further inspiration....

slate spiral

A striking treatment for a patio, small garden or an area within a bigger design. Using only pebbles and slate, it provides a dramatic backdrop for flowerbeds and decorative containers in addition to being wonderfully easy to maintain. As every space is different, it is impossible to give exact measurements or templates for this design, but the basic message is to keep it simple.

If you have a square or circular space, just use a spiral and ignore the 'tail' (such as the design on page 101). Alternatively, a longer, wider garden could have the spiral at one end with a wiggly 'tail' at the other.

slate spiral steps

materials

cement and coarse sand
blackboard chalk
white water-based paint
masonry nails
small blocks of wood,
  20 x 5 x 5cm (8 x 2 x 2in)
strips of ply, 2mm thick x 5cm
  wide (⅛ x 2in), to fit around
  the spiral shape
nails for wood
pebbles of varying colours
slate

equipment

paintbrush
hammer
spade for mixing cement
trowel
slate cutter
rubber mallet

⚠ Prepare the area to be pebbled by laying a flat, sound layer of cement. Slope the cement slightly away from the house and drill or leave drainage holes. Allow to dry thoroughly. Using chalk, draw a large spiral on the cement, starting in the middle working outwards.

◀2 Draw a second line approximately 20cm (8in) from, and parallel to, the first line. Taper each end of the shape.

3 When satisfied with the spiral shape, fill it in with white water-based paint. This will allow you to see the design clearly and to make any changes to the final design before starting to cement.

4 Using masonry nails, fix the small blocks of wood to the white-painted shape spacing them approximately every 10cm (4in). Each end of the block should sit on the white line. Do this for the whole of the white-painted shape.

5 Nail strips of ply to the side of the wooden blocks, starting on the inside of the shape. Attaching the strips in their centres and working outwards makes them easier to handle.

slate spiral 97

6 ▶ Now nail the ply strips to the outer edge of the blocks, finishing in the centre.

7 ▼ Working a section at a time, fill in an area with cement, starting in the middle of the spiral.

8 Press the pebbles in very firmly, lengthways down.

Slate has very sharp edges and can be extremely dangerous when placed on its edge, as it has been in this design. It is not suitable for areas where small children will

9 Continue to fill with cement and pebbles, making each section to the same level. Note that a row of black pebbles has been added to give extra interest in the middle of the design.

Keep the mosaic covered if there is any threat of rain. Completing a project of this size will inevitably mean working over several days. As a result there will be a join mark between each day's cement, but try to make it part of the pattern. Here, decorative lines have been set in the cement, running left to right.

10 Allow to dry for four to five days before walking on the pebbles. Remove the blocks and the ply. Using a slate cutter, cut the slate into long strips.

11 Fill the spiral area with a bed of sand approximately 2–3cm (¾–1¼in) deep.

slate spiral 99

12 Working at an angle across the spiral, fill with the slate strips inserted vertically, cutting them to fit as you work. Using a rubber mallet, tap into place so they are tightly packed and cannot become loose. Continue filling in until the whole shape is completed.

right: This spiral design can be tailored to fit any shape of garden. Here, a small square garden is enhanced by a simple, yet striking, circular spiral.

further inspiration...

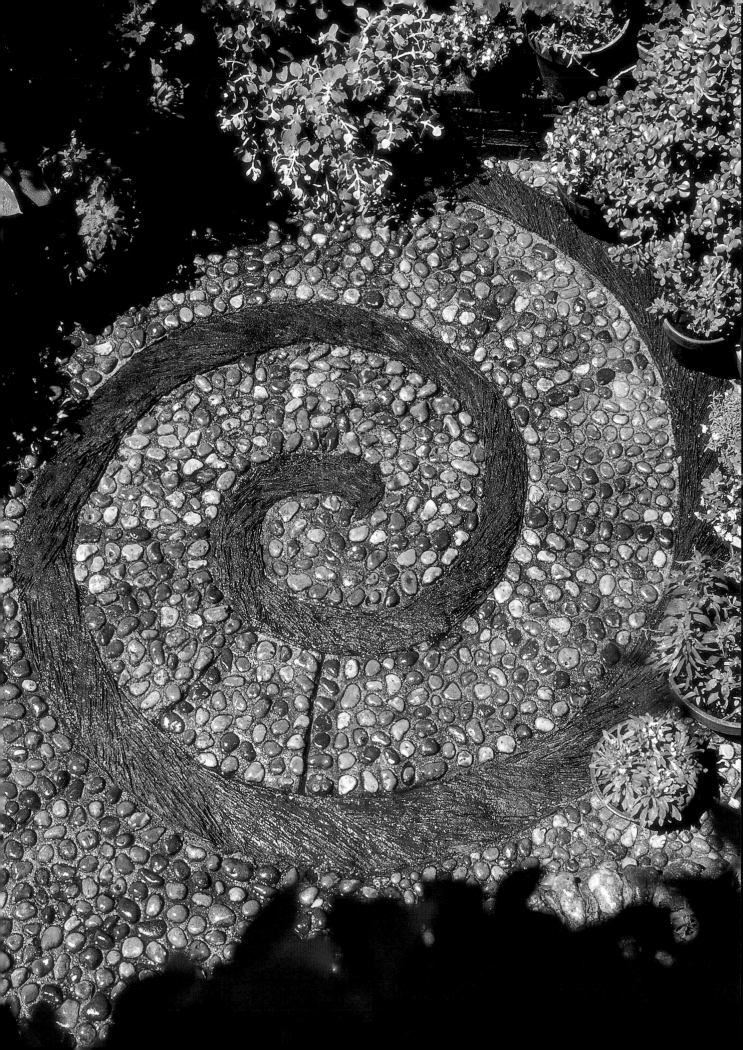

pebble essentials

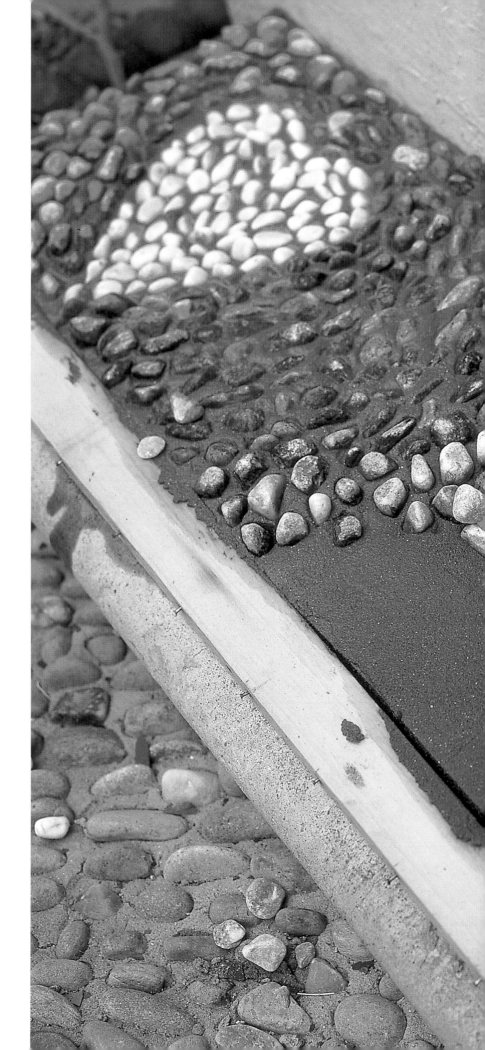

materials

pebbles These are very good for filling in background areas in larger designs. Beach and river pebbles are perfect for all mosaics, but do remember that it is illegal to remove them without permission. Quarries will often allow you to sort through piles of pebbles and select colours. Many garden suppliers sell pebbles. (See suppliers, pages 126–7.)

Try to acquire evenly shaped smooth pebbles and a variety of shapes. Colours vary enormously but be aware that contrast of colour is important.

special pebbles The 'stars' of many designs are pebbles that are particularly beautiful or strongly patterned. These should be collected and saved for features within a mosaic. (It is unlikely that anyone would object to the removal of one beach pebble for an 'eye' or other small detail.)

glass nuggets Round, dome-shaped clear and opaque glass nuggets come in a wide range of colours and are good for detail and interest. Remember to push them in deeply or they will pop out of the cement.

glass sea beans These glass 'pebbles' come in a wide variety of colours and closely resemble jelly beans in size and shape. They are excellent for mosaic due to their uniform colour and texture.

semi-precious stones Although these are much more expensive than ordinary pebbles they come in a lovely range of pastel colours and are ideal for a very special area within a mosaic.

beads Beads add extra detail. Glass beads are ideal.

glass pendants (donuts) Thick, flat, opaque discs of glass with a central hole. Available from bead shops.

glass disks Round flat disks of opaque glass. Inserted vertically, they are excellent for outlines. A limited variety of shades are available.

polished pebbles Readily available from garden suppliers and interior design stores, these come in a range of colours and contrast well with matt pebbles. The black ones look particularly dynamic.

slate The linear texture of slate, inserted vertically into cement, provides great contrast when added to an area of pebbles. Slate roofing tiles, cut into strips, are a useful addition to the mosaic pebbler's palette.

However, be extremely careful of its sharp edges, especially when it is used on its edge in a design: it is not suitable for areas where small children will run around barefoot.

mosaic tiles These are available in a vast range of colours in both glass and ceramic. Gold and silver are ideal for areas around an eye (see upstream, page 14), or another special area.

glass moons Fantastic for scales, feathers, petals and a host of other decorative additions to a mosaic. Available in a variety of colours.

Dutch metal Available in gold and silver, this comes in very thin sheet form and is available from good artists' suppliers. It is similar to gold and silver leaf but is much cheaper and easier to handle. It must be used with a tacky substance called size to adhere it to the relevant surface or material. Once it is attached, a coat of varnish prevents tarnishing.

metal size (wundersize) Size is used to make Dutch metal adhere to a surface. Paint it on the area to be gilded and leave to dry for at least 20 minutes until it is transparent. Dutch metal is then smoothed onto the sized area.

resin A liquid that comes in tins with a separate catalyst that is added to make it harden. Available from craft and hobby shops. Different brands may have required different methods or quantities, so be sure to follow the manufacturer's instructions.

shredded paper For making papier mâché. Do not use newspaper. Shredded office paper is perfect. For supplies, try friends or local recycling facilities.

PVA A white, water-soluble glue, available from art and craft shops.

copper sheet (shim) A thin metal sheet that also comes in pewter and brass. It is pliable and soft, and can be drawn on with a hard, pointed tool such as a biro. Do not confuse it with copper sheet from DIY stores, which is much thicker. Available from craft shops and mail-order outlets. (See suppliers, pages 126–7.)

plaster of Paris Available in craft shops and artists' suppliers. If possible, buy it in small bags as it has a limited life.

potter's clay Any potter's clay is suitable and is widely available from artists' shops. Keep it covered with plastic or a damp cloth to prevent it from drying out.

clingfilm Plastic film used in the kitchen. Invaluable for papier mâché.

varnish Water-based varnishes are ideal for everything except for varnishing the areas that have been gilded with Dutch metal sheet, for which you must use spirit-based varnish.

card This is used for transferring template shapes to the mosaic area. Any thick card is suitable.

cement (dry) Available from builders' merchants and DIY stores. Mixed with sharp sand and water to make wet cement for large areas. (See mixing cement, pages 110–111.)

ready-mixed sand/ cement A ready-made mixture of cement powder and sand can also be bought from builders' merchants and DIY stores. This is ideal for smaller projects. Just add water and mix to the manufacturer's instructions.

sharp sand Mixed with cement powder and water to make wet cement.

chicken wire This wire mesh is inserted into cement when wet, to reinforce it when it is dry. It is available with holes of different sizes – choose a small-hole type with holes approximately 1cm (½in) wide.

wooden boards Used for pictures, and for making frames in which to cast cement. Use blockboard, MDF (medium density fiberboard) or thick ply, not hardboard (which will disintegrate when wet).

nails/screws Size depends on the particular project. Masonry nails are designed to fix into cement.

paint Water-based paint is used for decorating the bases of pebble mosaics, whether plaster, cement or papier mâché. Gold metallic paint can also be used.

glasspaper More commonly known as sandpaper. Use a fine grade for distressing gilded areas or smoothing rough edges of plaster or wood.

proprietary cement cleaner If your finished work is marked by unwanted smears of cement, this cleaner can be employed to remove them.

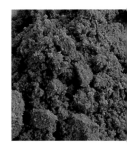

chalk Draw your design on a cement surface with ordinary blackboard chalk. Errors can be removed or changes made by wiping or washing it off.

equipment

designing

pencil For marking out designs and shapes on both paper and wooden board.

ruler Useful for measuring and providing a hard edge.

tape measure A builders' steel tape is essential for measuring and marking out larger designs.

string Can be used for marking out a curve or circle.

ballpoint pen An ideal tool for embossing designs onto metal sheet.

scissors Sharp scissors are used for cutting paper, thick card and, for some projects, metal sheet.

artist's brushes A variety of brushes are useful for applying size, painting and varnishing.

woodwork

saw or jigsaw Some projects require wooden frames in which to cast cement shapes. A jigsaw makes light work of cutting curves.

drill and drill bits Screw holes are needed for assembling wooden frames.

trowel An essential tool for mixing and laying cement.

spirit level A long spirit level is essential to check the levels of slabs in outdoor projects.

skewer or pointed stick Useful for drawing in cement.

wire cutters Used for cutting chicken wire. Strong scissors will do the same job.

face mask Always wear a protective mask when mixing cement or resin.

soft paintbrush Use an old brush to fill in gaps between blocks of cement.

screwdriver

hammer

tiles and slate

tile cutter A domestic tile cutter, available from DIY stores, will cut mosaic tiles and thin slate.

slate cutter If large quantities of slate must be cut for a garden design, a substantial slate cutter will make the job much easier.

rubber mallet When laying designs of vertical slate sheets, use this tool to pack the slate in densely (see slate spiral, page 94).

papier mâché

measuring jug Helpful when quantities of liquid have to be measured (also useful when working with resin).

saucepan For boiling paper when making papier mâché.

liquidizer/blender One of these kitchen machines is invaluable for making papier mâché.

sieve or colander Use a kitchen implement when draining papier-mâché pulp.

rolling pin Papier-mâché pulp must be rolled flat before it can be used.

plastic spreader or corraflute Either of these can be used for smoothing papier-mâché pulp.

Corraflute (a lightweight plastic sheet) can be found in art and craft shops.

basic techniques

mixing cement

Cement is a mix of cement powder, sand and water. The dry components can either be bought separately, or ready mixed in a bag. Ready-mixed sand and cement is convenient and quick for smaller projects. Cement and sand mixed separately is more suitable – and more economical – for larger projects such as steps, paths and gardens. For large quantities it is probably easiest to mix it with a spade, using an old piece of hardboard as a mixing surface.

Alternatively, for major projects such as a garden, you may even wish to hire an electric mixer.

⚠ If using ready-mixed cement, empty the dry mix into a large tray or bucket. If the cement and sand have been bought separately, add four parts sharp sand to one part cement.

◀2 Before adding water, stir thoroughly to mix the sand and cement.

3 Add water to ready-mixed cement according to the manufacturer's instructions. However, simply add enough water to cement and sand to make a thick consistency.

4 Mix the cement mixture and water thoroughly to reach the desired consistency.

tip

For a large project, make up the cement in batches, so that it does not have a chance to go off before all the pebbles are inserted. This will be determined by the weather: obviously cement will dry faster on a warm, dry day than it will on a cool damp one.

tip

Make sure the surface of the pebble mosaic is even; use a board or plank to tamp down the surface.

tip

If water forms on the surface of the cement as you start work, mop a little up with a paper towel. (Do not make it bone dry.) When you start pushing in the pebbles, the water will gradually begin to disappear.

tip

The pebbles should be well pushed into the cement – to at least half their depth or 1.5cm (⅝in) – otherwise they will come out or, if outside, will be pushed out by frost. Pebbles should be pushed in lengthways where possible.

mixing plaster

materials

plaster of Paris
water
mixing bowl

1 Pour water into the bowl. Put a handful of plaster into the middle of the water. Do not stir.

2 Continue to add a handful at a time (always in the middle) until a dry peak appears rising out of the water (which looks a little like a volcano). Add one more handful.

3 Stir with your hand until the mixture has the consistency of thin cream. Stir a few more times and pour into the mould, tapping the side of the mould to dispel air bubbles.

tip

It is important to remember that plaster of Paris has a relatively short shelf life. If you have an old bag, throw it away and get a new one.

tip

As the plaster sets and hardens it gives off heat. This is quite normal.

making papier mâché

materials

shredded paper
saucepan
liquidizer
sieve or colander
PVA glue
bowl

1 Put a large quantity of shredded paper into a saucepan. Add a large quantity of water and boil vigorously for at least 20 minutes until the fibres begin to break up. Leave to cool.

2 Liquidize the paper and some of the water until the shreds have completely broken up. Switching the machine on and off ('pulsing') will help this process.

3 Using your hands, squeeze out as much excess water as possible. Drain the pulp through a sieve or a colander.

4 Add the PVA glue to the pulp at a rate of approximately one cup to a small mixing bowl full of pulp. The pulp should hold together easily without leaving a glue residue on the hands. Mix well.

tip
If the pulp won't hold together, add more PVA glue. If it is sticky on your hands, add more pulp.

tip
Papier mâché pulp can be kept for several days if tied up in a plastic bag to prevent it from drying out.

templates

upstream p14
enlarge 200%

silver fish   p20

enlarge 200%

heart mirror p26

enlarge 200%

mirror
area

pure pebbles p32
actual size

daisy hearth p44
enlarge 200%

topiary tree p58

enlarge 400%

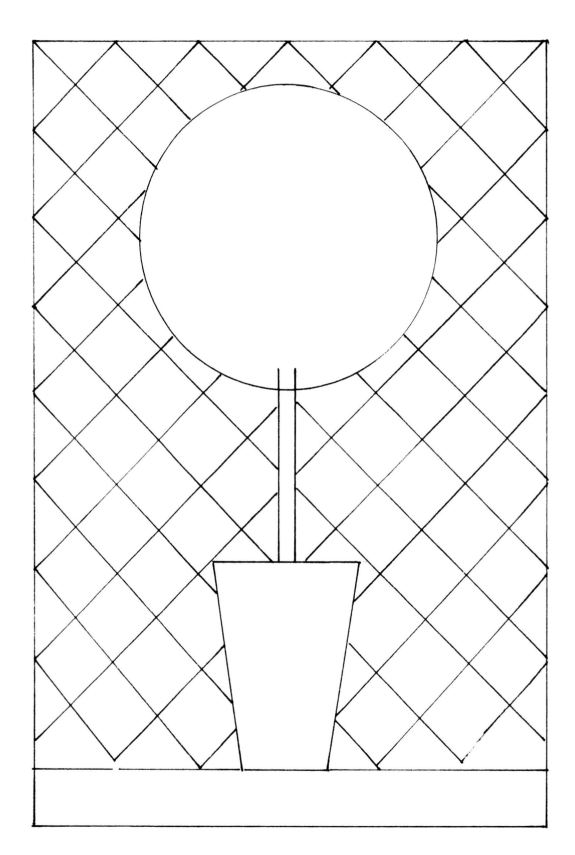

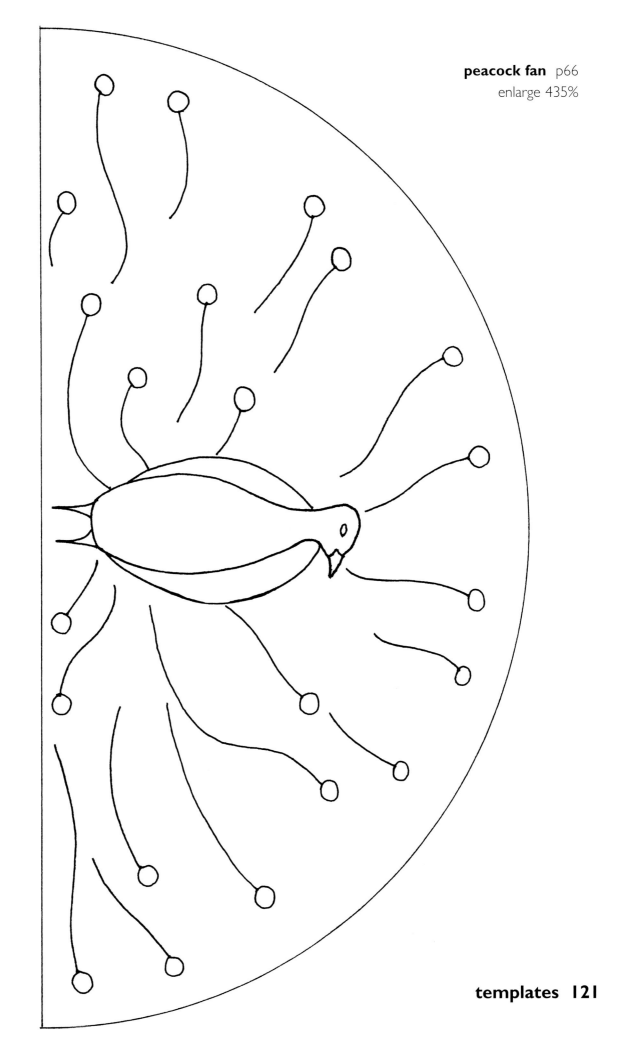

fountain swirl
copper fish p74
actual size

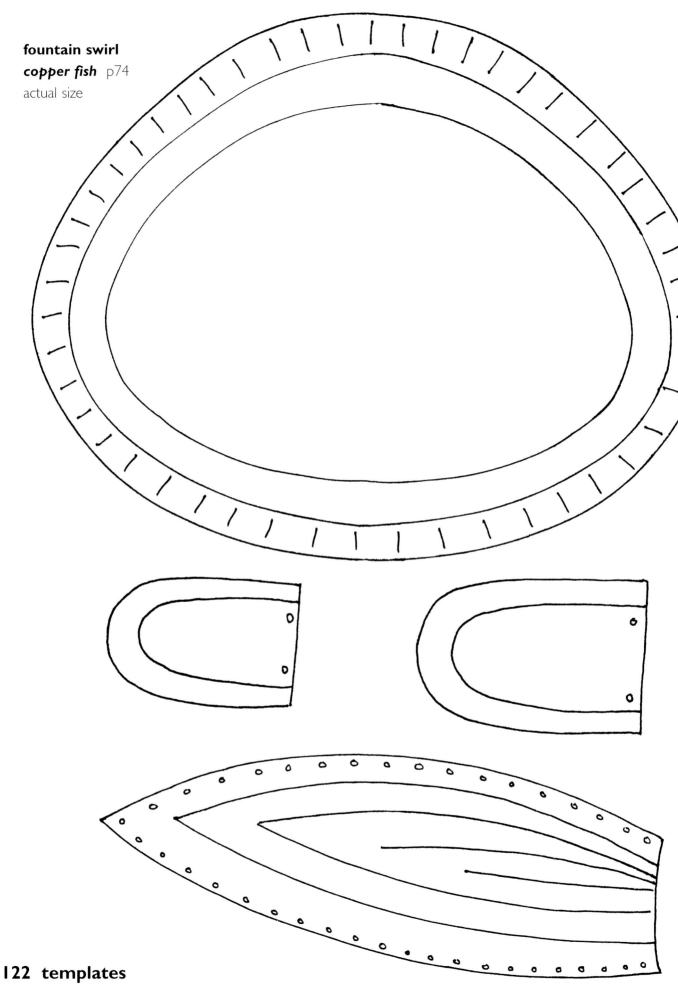

fountain swirl

outer mosaic p79

enlarge 300%

oriental path
diamond p84
actual size

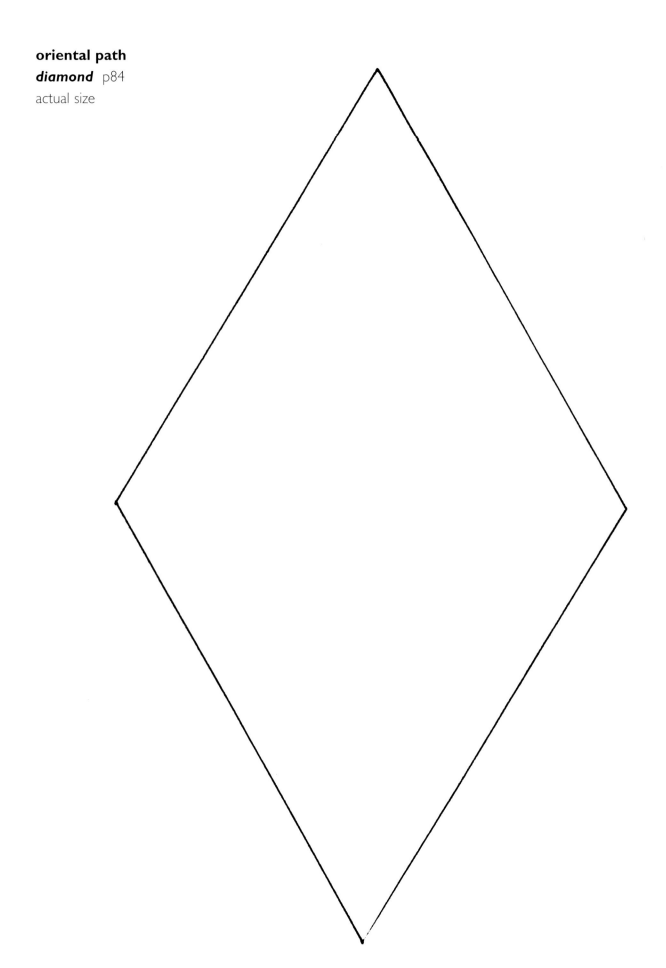

oriental path

star p88

enlarge 400%

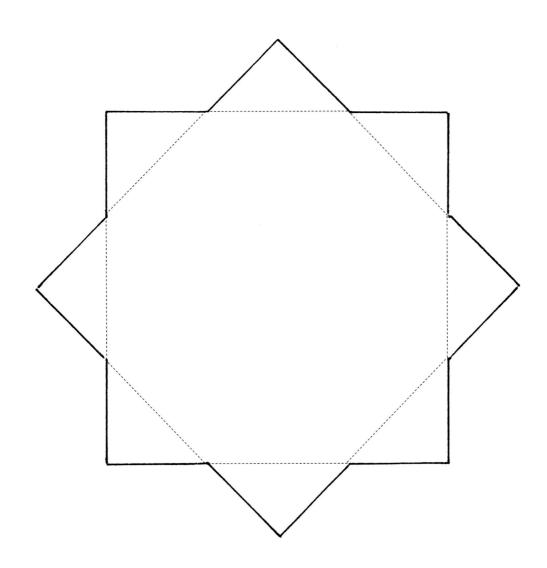

suppliers

UK

B&Q DIY and Garden Supercentres
nationwide chain
pebbles

The Brighton Bead Shop
21 Sydney Street
Brighton
East Sussex BN1 4EN
tel: 01273 675077
website: www.beadsunlimited.co.uk
beads, glass pendants (donuts)
mail order

British Fossils
Unit 2,
Bailey Gate Industrial Estate
Sturminster Marshall
Wimborne
Dorset BH21 4DB
email: sales@britishfossils.co.uk
semi-precious stones

Castlecary Depot
Allandale
By Bonnybridge
Scotland FK4 2HJ
tel: 01773 769916
pebbles, slate

**Civil Engineering
Developments Ltd (CED)**
728 London Road
West Thurrock
Grays
Essex RM20 3LU
tel: 01708 867237
large range of pebbles, slate, marble etc.
also at:
Midlands
East View Terrace
Langly Mill
Notts NG16 4DF

Country Gardens
nationwide chain of garden centres
wide range of Borderstone pebbles

Economy of Brighton
82 St George's Road
Kemp Town
Brighton
East Sussex BN2 1EF
tel: 01273 682831
website: www.economyofbrighton.co.uk
PVA glue, paint, clay, Dutch metal, size
mail order

The Guilders Warehouse
5&4D Woodside Commercial Estate
Thornwood
Epping
Essex CM16 6LJ
tel: 01992 570453
fax: 01992 561320
Dutch metal, size
mail order

House of Marbles
Pottery Road
Bovey Tracey
Devon TQ13 9DS
tel: 01626 835358
website: www.houseofmarbles.com
*glass nuggets, sea glass, beach glass,
moons, stars etc.*
mail order

Plastic Merchants Ltd
10 Church Street
Brighton
East Sussex BN1 1IS
tel: 01273 329958
clear casting resin and moulds

Southern Handicrafts
20 Kensington Gardens
Brighton
East Sussex BN1 4AL
tel: 01273 681901
website: www.southernhandicrafts.co.uk
metal sheet (shim), resin, glass mosaic tiles

US

Art2Art
432 Culver Boulevard
Playa Del Rey
CA 90203
tel: (877) 427 2383
fax: (310) 827 8111
assorted craft supplies, including metals

Home Depot, USA, Inc
2455 Paces Ferry Road
Atlanta
GA 30339-4024
tel: (770) 433 8211
website: www.homedepot.com
*home improvement store with more than 1,000
locations in the USA, Canada and abroad – check the
store locator on the website for the nearest location*

House of Marbles
PO Box 5814
11–13 Ilene Court
Hillsborough
NJ 08844
tel: (908) 281 9158
website: www.houseofmarbles.com
*glass nuggets, sea glass, beach glass,
moons, stars etc.*
mail order

Paragona Art Products
1150 18th Street, Suite 200
Santa Monica
CA 90403
tel: (310) 264 1980
supplier of soft copper sheet

Wits End Mosaics
5224 West State Road 46
Suite 134
Sanford, FL 32771
tel: (407) 32 9122
fax: (407) 322 8552
website: www.mosaic-witsend.com
email: info@mosaic-witsend.com
*glass gems, smalti and assorted shapes and
colours of tile*

acknowledgments

Special thanks to the following:

Chris Markwick for his patience with

endless pebbles; Alison Myer for help,

support and guidance on marsupial

costume choices; Stewart Grant for making

the photography look fab, and Jerry Lebens

for his help with the Slate Spiral and

Oriental Path photographs; Jane Hawkins

for all her help and encouragement;

Kate and Nick for the use of their garden;

Lindsay Porter for help and encouragement;

Margot Richardson for a grand job, and

most of all to the lovely Simon Arnold

for everything.

Visit the author's website at
www.annfrith.co.uk

index

Illustrations shown in *italic*